Jemima Puddle-Duck and her Friends Coloring Book

From the original and authorized stories
by Beatrix Potter
F. Warne & Co.

She tried to hide her eggs; but they were always found and carried off.
The Tale of Jemima Puddle-Duck

She ran downhill a few yards flapping her shawl, and then she jumped into the air.
The Tale of Jemima Puddle-Duck

The shed was almost quite full of feathers—
it was almost suffocating; but it was comfortable and very soft.
The Tale of Jemima Puddle-Duck

When she came out, the sandy-whiskered gentleman
was sitting on a log reading the newspaper.
The Tale of Jemima Puddle-Duck

The foxy gentleman admired the eggs immensely.
He used to turn them over and count them
when Jemima was not there.
The Tale of Jemima Puddle-Duck

Presently Kep opened the door of the shed,
and let out Jemima Puddle-Duck.
The Tale of Jemima Puddle-Duck

Tom Kitten was very fat, and he had grown;
several buttons burst off. His mother sewed them on again.
The Tale of Tom Kitten

When the three kittens were ready, Mrs. Tabitha unwisely
turned them out into the garden.
The Tale of Tom Kitten

But he put the clothes on *himself!*
They fitted him even worse than Tom Kitten.
The Tale of Tom Kitten

He was quite pleased when he looked out and saw large drops of rain, splashing in the pond.
The Tale of Mr. Jeremy Fisher

The boat was round and green and very like the other lily leaves.
The Tale of Mr. Jeremy Fisher

And instead of a nice dish of minnows—they had roasted grasshopper with lady-bird sauce.

The Tale of Mr. Jeremy Fisher

Nutkin sat upon a big flat rock, and played ninepins with a crab apple and green fir-cones.
The Tale of Squirrel Nutkin

'Shuh! shuh! little dirty feet!' said Mrs. Tittlemouse, clattering her dust-pan.
The Tale of Mrs. Tittlemouse

And one day a little old woman ran up and down
in a spotty red cloak.
The Tale of Mrs. Tittlemouse

When she got back to the parlour,
she heard some one coughing in a fat voice;
and there sat Mr. Jackson himself!

The Tale of Mrs. Tittlemouse

Then she went out, and fetched some twigs,
to partly close up the front door.
The Tale of Mrs. Tittlemouse

She rubbed up the furniture with beeswax,
and polished her little tin spoons.
The Tale of Mrs. Tittlemouse

Little Benjamin Bunny slid down into the road, and set off—
with a hop, skip and a jump—to call upon his relations.
The Tale of Benjamin Bunny

In the neatest, sandiest hole of all,
lived Benjamin's aunt and his cousins—
Flopsy, Mopsy, Cotton-Tail and Peter.
The Tale of Benjamin Bunny

Peter described how he had been chased about the garden,
and had dropped his shoes and coat.
The Tale of Benjamin Bunny

Presently Peter dropped half the onions.
The Tale of Benjamin Bunny

Goody Tiptoes was busy pushing moss under the thatch.
The Tale of Timmy Tiptoes

They began to empty the bags into a hole high up a tree,
that had belonged to a woodpecker.
The Tale of Timmy Tiptoes

Next time Goody brought another bagful,
a little striped chipmunk scrambled out in a hurry.
The Tale of Timmy Tiptoes

She led the way to the woodpecker's tree,
and they listened at the hole.
The Tale of Timmy Tiptoes

When Benjamin Bunny grew up, he married his cousin Flopsy.
They had a large family.
The Tale of the Flopsy Bunnies

They could hear him drag his chair on the flags, and chuckle—
'One, two, three, four, five, six leetle rabbits!' said Mr. McGregor.
The Tale of the Flopsy Bunnies

Opposite to him—as far away as he could sit—
was an enormous rat.
The Tale of Samuel Whiskers

Samuel Whiskers went boldly down the front staircase to the dairy to get the butter.
The Tale of Samuel Whiskers

There are rats, and rats, and rats in his barn!
They eat up the chicken food, and steal the oats and bran,
and make holes in the meal bags.
The Tale of Samuel Whiskers